CAT TRAINING

BECAUSE CAT IS SIMPLY CAT
HOW TO UNDERSTAND – TRAIN – EDUCATE YOUR CAT

PLETL

This book is protected by copyright!

Contact

Pletl
Tsar Ivaylo 12
9101 Byala
Bulgaria

feedback-book@hotmail.com

ISBN: 9798525472501

Exclusion of liability

This book has been written to provide information. Every effort has been made to make this book as complete and accurate as possible. However, it may contain typographical or content errors. Furthermore, this book contains information only up to the date of publication. Therefore, this book should be used as a guide and not as a definitive source. The purpose of this book is to enlighten. The author and publisher do not guarantee the completeness of the information contained in this book and assume no liability for errors or omissions.
The author and publisher accept no liability for any loss or damage caused or alleged to be caused directly or indirectly by this book.

FOREWORD

I disagree with the saying that dogs are man's best friend. Not that I have anything against dogs; they are amazing animals and their loyalty is legendary. I just have a thing for cats. No, wait...let me rephrase that. I am absolutely crazy and have an obsessive passion for cats. They are the most captivating, mysterious, intelligent and loving creatures you can find. Furthermore, they are also super cute and cuddly. Anyone who has befriended a cat will agree that it is a very special bond and a unique friendship.

I can't remember a time when we had less than 10 cats sharing our home and garden. We have welcomed several new litters into the world, nursed sick cats back to health, taken in adorable strays and loved each and every one of them. Sadly, we have also experienced the heartbreaking loss of several of our beloved little ones. The love and affection we shared with our pets were more than worth it. Of course, caring for a cat and maintaining a clean, tidy living space takes some time and effort. Over the years, I have learned how to do this through a lot of testing. We now have a system that we are pretty good with. My cats are well behaved, well behaved (most of the time!), in good health and as happy as can be. Now I have decided to share all my knowledge about cats with you.

What this book offers

If you are reading this book, you either already have a cat or are considering adopting one. If you are in the first category, congratulations! If you are in the second category, go for it! However, as a pet owner, there are two things you should keep in mind. First, that you give your pet the care it needs to live a long, happy and healthy life. Secondly, you want to make sure your cat is well behaved to save you both a lot of trouble later on.

Cats are creatures of habit. Once they have developed a certain behaviour, it is very difficult to break them of it. So the secret is to teach them good habits early on. But it's never too late to teach an old cat new tricks!
Training and caring for a cat is a fairly simple and straightforward process. This book will reflect that simplicity by teaching you the basics of holistic cat care through a series of simple but effective methods.

You will also gain amazing insights into the world of cats, including how to understand your cat's behaviour and language, their unique traits and how to use this knowledge to care for your kitty and give them the best care and nutrition. More importantly, you will learn what not to do, as I have learned from my years of experience.

The book is a representation of all the "best cat practices" that exist. We have tried them all and picked out the ones that really work. Hopefully, by the time you've finished reading, you'll be armed with some important (and surprising) insights about your pet.

Ultimately, sharing your life with a cat is about developing an amazing relationship that brings enormous joy into both your lives. This book will help you achieve that.

THE HISTORY
OF THE
DOMESTIC CAT

Today, millions of cats live happily with humans around the world. In the United States alone, 47 million households own cats, an average of two per household. Where, how and when did the history of the domestic cat - and the love story with humans - begin?
Here is a brief history of how cats became one of the most popular pets in the world.

Science is not able to tell us conclusively how or when cats were domesticated. The skeletons of feral and domesticated cats are very similar, which is a challenge for archaeologists. However, it is estimated that domestication began 20,000 years ago when feral cats began to make their way into primitive villages, possibly in search of food.

What the archaeological record shows beyond doubt is that cats have lived with humans since the dawn of civilisation. Some scientists estimate this to be around 8,000 to 10,000 years. Others suggest that the relationship began as early as 14,000 years ago.

Most scientists agree that today's cats are descended from the North African wild cat, which was very adaptable to all kinds of habitats, allowing the species to reproduce and spread all over the world.

The most popular theory of how cats became domesticated is also the most plausible. When people discovered agriculture, they began to settle near fertile riverbanks. Their crops attracted rodents and snakes, which in turn attracted wild cats to the villages. The cats had plenty of easy prey and the people had rodent-free fields. This relationship was so beneficial for both species that they decided to live together - and the rest is history!

The symbiotic relationship between cats and humans evolved over the centuries into mutual friendship and companionship. There is strong evidence from many ancient cultures that cats were raised as beloved pets. The most significant discovery in this regard was made in 2004 by archaeologist Jean-Denis Vigne.

In an ancient burial site in Cyprus, he discovered the remains of a cat buried next to its owner. The remains date back to 750 B.C. The discovery sheds important light on the domestication of cats as pets and companions at a very early stage in history.

The ancient Egyptians built the pyramids. This amazing achievement overshadows the fact that they were passionate cat lovers. Cats were revered, cherished and even worshipped by the ancient Egyptians. Thousands of temple carvings bear witness to the fact that cats ruled Egypt! Hundreds of statues and thousands of mummified cats excavated by archaeologists reflect the high status of the domestic cat. Mummification was performed on humans to preserve the body for passage into the afterlife and rebirth. The fact that the ancient Egyptians did the same with their cats shows that they were valued so much that their owners wanted to be reunited with them after death.

The era of the Middle Ages is sometimes called the Dark Ages - and very rightly so, in my opinion. This was a time when harmonious relationships took a wild and sinister turn. Cats were now associated with witchcraft, black magic and devil worship. The black cat, previously worshipped as a loving goddess in ancient Egypt, became an incarnation of Satan. The result was a cruel rampage in which cats were killed, tortured and burned alive. The cruel crusade continued throughout Europe until by the 16th century cats were virtually extinct.

Fast forward to the 20th century, where we find that cats have become pets. Along with dogs, they are the pets of choice in many cultures around the world.

Final thoughts:

Perhaps the most significant achievement of the 20th century was the growing awareness of animal welfare. Today, cats are protected by law from all forms of mistreatment and abuse. Many organisations around the world are working diligently to ensure the humane treatment of animals and to protect their rights. Isn't it good to know that your cat has legal rights? And aren't you glad that we live in the 21st century?

CAN CATS BE
TRAINED AT ALL?

Here's a fact that I hate to admit, as inclined as I am towards cats: It's easier to train dogs than cats. It's not that cats are less intelligent; it's just that dogs respond to training with more excitement and motivation. They enjoy the challenge of learning new things, especially tricks.

Cats are extremely intelligent and inquisitive and can learn just as quickly as dogs - they just aren't as interested. They are very happy to go with the flow and may not welcome interference or attempts to change the status quo. To be honest, cats can be stubborn as hell! Their defiant independence is part of what makes them so lovable. When it comes to training, this can be a challenge for you.

Let me assure you that cats can definitely be trained and taught a variety of habits and behaviours. This can be done by playing with their natural curiosity and through rewards and positive reinforcement.

Education vs. training

When we use the term "training" in relation to cats, it should really mean education. The goal is to train your cat to adapt to the customs and schedule of your household and daily routine. It also means helping your cat to develop a set of good habits and behaviours. The goal should not really be to teach a cat to stand on its hind legs, wave goodbye or retrieve a ball. Of course cats can learn to do these things and more, and there is no rule against teaching them. But honestly, the only purpose here would be to have fun and show your friends how smart your pet is. Believe me, if you leave your cat to its own devices, it will come up with many more amusing and adorable antics than you can ever teach it. So make sure your smartphone is always handy to capture these moments on video. Your main goal in training your cat should be to help her learn how to adapt to your lifestyle, how to stay safe and healthy, and how to behave in certain situations. Let me give you an example. When it was feeding time at our house, everyone passing by outside thought that some form of horrible mass torture was going on inside.

Our cats went wild when it was time for them to be fed. They screamed, scratched, jumped on worktops and basically just went crazy. This is normal behaviour in some cats and not a sign that something is wrong. It actually started with one, but quickly spread to the other three well-behaved cats (does the term "copycat" sound familiar)? Even my angelic, aptly named Fairy jumped on my back, climbed over my shoulder and jumped onto the kitchen worktop.

When feeding the cats became a dreaded, nerve-wracking task, I did some research and was able to teach the little rebels to stay calm and patient at mealtimes. That's the kind of training that's worth the effort.
Some other things you can teach your cat are, for example,

not to bite too hard when playing with you or other cats, to walk on a leash outside or to stay calm during car rides. In other words, training your cat is more about teaching everyday behaviours and making these habits permanent. Now that we have established that cats can be trained, let's look at some basic cat training facts that you should consider.

- Cats have a short attention span. This, combined with their natural stubbornness, means that training sessions need to be short.

- Cats are not motivated by treats. Sure, they eat the treat, but then go back to licking their paws and ignoring you completely.

- Every cat is unique and has individual preferences and characteristics. Training should be adapted according to their reactions.

- Training a cat requires more patience and gentleness than training a dog.

- The training sessions should be short and last no longer than 10-15 minutes.

- Cats can learn to respond to gestures and words

- Rewards can be anything from a treat to a warm petting session. It's up to you to find out what your cat prefers.

The quintessence

Every cat is different. Her independent character, breed and age have an influence on how quickly she will learn. It also depends on your knowledge of cat behaviour so that you can correctly interpret your cat's reactions. You will learn all about this in a later chapter.

Finally, training your cat can be something you both look forward to and enjoy if you exercise patience. It's loving work that will be worth it when you and your cat reap the first rewards.

UNDERSTANDING
CAT LANGUAGE

You don't have to be an expert to understand your cat's language and interpret its behaviour. Cats may have individual personalities and quirks, but fortunately their language and behaviour is more or less the same across all breeds, shapes and sizes. Understanding your cat's language will give you a fascinating insight into their thoughts and feelings, which will help you calibrate training. More importantly, you learn how to respond to your pet's moods and become alert to unnatural behaviour that needs attention. In a way, your cat is also training you!

The body language of your cat

Cats rely more on body language than vocal expression to convey their message. Pay attention to the following nuances in your pet:

The ears

- The normal position of a cat's ears is when they are slightly bent forward. It means that your cat is relaxed and that all is well with its world.

- If the ears are perked up and standing at attention, this signals that the cat is angry or fearful. If the ears are pointed and twitching, it means that an unknown noise is making your pet suspicious.

- If your cat's ears are straight up and stiff, he wants to play. Now, this position is similar to the previous one, so it can be difficult to know if your pet is fearful, angry or playful. You should rely on additional signals such as the tail and eyes for clarification.

- Floppy ears mean your cat is relaxed and comfortable

- When a cat pulls back its ears and lays them flat, it senses danger or is in aggression mode. This is usually accompanied by hissing and often occurs when cats are about to fight.

The tail

- A limp, relaxed tail is a sign that your cat is comfortable and relaxed.

- If you notice your cat's tail twitching or swinging back and forth, you can be sure she is thinking about mischief! She is in a very playful mood. A cat will also twitch her tail when she sees birds, squirrels or mice. In this case, she goes into "playful predator" mode.

- If your pet walks around with its tail held high and curled up, you know it is feeling extra good and happy.

- If your cat sits with its tail pressed close to its body, this may be a sign of anxiety. However, many cats prefer this position, so it is up to you to interpret the sign depending on the situation.

- A bristly, fluffed tail means that a cat is anxious.

The eyes

- When your cat starts to blink slowly and purr, you know she's over the moon!

- Cats typically have bouts of manic play where they suddenly chase their own tails, jump in the air or do all sorts of crazy acrobatics. You can anticipate this by noticing your cat's dilated pupils,

- Dilated pupils can also signal anger or fear, so again it is up to you to assess the situation.

- Constricted pupils are a sign that your pet is scared.

Kneading

Kneading is a secretive action that most cats perform where they slide their paws in and out on a soft surface. The action resembles kneading bread and hence the name.

Not all cats do this, but it is a habit that is innate to them. You will notice that baby kittens purr and knead at mummy's tummy when they are suckling. Some cats continue this habit as adults, while others do not. I have noticed that female cats do this more often. Some cats knead with their claws, which can be quite uncomfortable if they do this on your lap.

So, what does kneading mean? There are several theories, but none of them are conclusive. Suffice it to say that your cat is happy when it kneads!

The vocal utterances of your cat

Meowing

What's in a meow? More than you can imagine. A cat's meow is a complex form of communication that can tell you a lot because it is specifically for you.

Here's a fascinating fact: Cats meow to communicate with humans! Cats communicate with each other through smell, touch and body language. But they're so smart that they've figured out that we're different and that the only way to get through to us is to make noises like us. So the next time your cat gets noisy, here's what it might be telling you:

- A long-drawn-out meow when you come home means that your cat is happy to see you - or that it is scolding you for being away too long. I think it's more the latter!

- A long, loud meow means your little friend wants some attention.

- A short, clipped meow actually means "hello"! We had a cat who, whenever she came into the house from the garden, would give this short meow and run to her basket to take a nap. Now that I know it's a "hello", I always return the greeting.

- A high-pitched meow signals distress or injury. Cats do this when they are getting ready to fight each other or when they have been injured.

Purr

We all know that a purring cat is a sign of a contented, happy cat, right? Well, not always. Purring can be a sign of two very different emotions in your cat.

If you have ever accompanied a cat at birth, you may have noticed that she purrs loudly. When I first experienced this with my cat Ginny, I was confused. Giving birth is a painful ordeal, even for cats. So why was Ginny purring so contentedly? My romantic mind came up with the idea that maybe she was looking forward to welcoming her new babies. But the frantic meowing that punctuated the purring told me she was in pain.

To make a long story short: Cats purr when they are happy and content - but they also purr when they are in distress. A cat also purrs when it is sick or injured or in shock, as a form of self-soothing.
So always make sure your pet is purring for the right reasons.

Snarl

Snarling, growling and scratching mean that your cat is in a hostile mood. This is a common behaviour in cats when they meet strangers, dogs or other cats.
It is very rare for your cat to hiss at you, but if it does, it could be a sign of illness or internal injury.

The bottom line: Cats can sometimes be quite mysterious, and in fact their behaviour is still being studied and observed through countless studies. We can expect that these studies will reveal more than we already know.
For now, your cat's body language, vocal cues and behaviour offer a wealth of insight into your cat's moods and feelings.

Start observing your furry friend and see how she reacts to certain situations and even to other cats. You will very quickly learn her likes and dislikes, which will lead to a stronger relationship.

CAT OR CAT? THE DIFFERENCES

Male and female cats are created equal. They are equally friendly, lovable and make the best pets. However, there are some behavioural differences between males and females that you should know in order to better understand your pet's behaviour.

A word of warning: these general differences are not always shown by all cats. More importantly, they have more to do with hormones than specific male or female personality traits. For example, people tend to think that males are more aggressive and aloof, while females are more gentle and affectionate. This is absolutely not true!

I've known female cats who fought with everything and everyone and didn't like petting. I've had male cats who were as docile and affectionate as angels and could spend all day in my lap purring contentedly. So use the information here to expand your cat knowledge, but don't be surprised if your pet's behaviour is completely different. You will also find the answer to the question of whether the behaviour of male or female cats should influence your choice if you are planning to adopt a cat.

It's all about hormones!

The basic differences are mainly influenced by the way Mother Nature created all cats. It is the basic, instinctive urge to breed. Here are some of the behaviours you can expect.

Behaviour of the male cat

Unneutered males are almost uncontrollable when the urge to mate seizes them. They only have one thing on their mind, so to speak, which blinds them to everything else. Male cats have been known to scratch sturdy bars on doors and windows to get in or out, depending on where a female cat is.

They have been known to make death-defying leaps out of windows and off balconies when females are around. I have a friend whose cat jumped from a third floor balcony and broke her leg. Keep an eye on your cat at this stage and take the necessary safety precautions to prevent such dangerous acrobatics.

You can expect the following behaviour from unneutered male cats:

- They mark their territory, which means they spray everywhere.

- He is eager to go outside in search of a female when there is none in the house.

- Being absent. Male cats in heat are often gone for days when they come outside. But they are usually around to woo a female, and when they are used to being let out, they find their way back home. The first time this happened to me, I spent several sleepless nights imagining the worst. Three days later he reappeared, cool as a cucumber, devoured a bowl of cat food, bathed himself thoroughly and curled up in his basket. Your cat will most likely return safe and sound, so give it a few days before worrying.

- Male cats fight and show aggression towards other male rivals

- Your pet may have no appetite and lose interest in playing or cuddling with you.

These behaviours will disappear or decrease significantly when you neuter your male cat. You can expect the following:

- He will play with other pedigree cats and be friendly. Fights become much less frequent and usually do not go beyond a few angry meows.

- He will make friends with both male and female cats and form special friendships with one or two.

- He only sprays when he is harassed or upset.

- He will be more cuddly and affectionate.

I have one piece of advice about neutering; call it more my personal opinion. Allow your cat to mate before you do so. There is no scientific support for or against it and of course necessity dictates that we neuter our cats and we should be grateful that the procedure is simple, safe and painless.

-

However, you can't help feeling that we are somehow defying nature or playing God. I always feel better when I have let my cats a few times and experience the full range of what they were created for.

Female cat behaviour

Females are a little more romantic than their male counterparts when unsprayed. They then show the following behaviour:

- She rolls onto her back and purrs and wants you to stroke her belly.

- Females can vocalise loudly when they are in heat.

- She wants to be stroked and cuddled and is very affectionate.

- Fights with rival females can occur.

- If there is a cat around, she takes the mating position, but sometimes, if there is no cat around, she will do the same to you! My teenage son always finds this extremely embarrassing!

- Your cat may become a little aggressive when she is in heat and there are no males around. This is because she feels frustrated.

When your pet is neutered, their behaviour will change as follows:

- She will no longer meow as loudly or be as affectionate as she was when she was in heat. However, she will still be cuddly and affectionate with you and other male and female friends.

- She will be a little suspicious of strange animals and people.

- Unlike neutered males, she does not like playfulness or rough antics and prefers rather calm behaviour.

- She may tend to befriend male cats more than females.

- She becomes very affectionate and shows her maternal side with small kittens

As with pedigree cats, I prefer to let a female cat have at least one litter and experience the joys of motherhood. The maternal instinct remains strong in most cats, even after they have been neutered. As I mentioned earlier, they tend to be very loving and caring with kittens.

I think if the instinct is that strong, a female cat should experience motherhood first hand. You can decide whether you want to keep the litter or put it up for adoption.

It can be a bit chaotic in the house for a while, but I think it's totally worth it. Sharing the experience of motherhood with your cat and her pride in her babies creates a very special bond.

Final thoughts

Does it really matter if you want to adopt a male or a female cat? The main difference is in the instinctive behaviour related to mating and not really much else. There may also be some behavioural differences after a cat has been neutered, but again they are negligible.

So are there personality differences? The answer is a resounding yes. But it has nothing to do with whether your cat is male or female. Just like people, each individual cat has its own unique characteristics and behaviours that simply make it special.

So if you are considering adopting a cat, don't think about males or females. Your first priority should always be the cat itself, which needs a warm, loving home the most.

A CAT FRIENDLY
ATTITUDE

A friendly, affectionate cat starts with you! And since you already have a cat or are considering adopting one, you love cats. You have already taken the first step.
Raising a friendly cat is as easy as these simple tips:

Train them to respond to your call

Your clever cat will quickly recognise its name if you repeat it often. Call your cat's name when it is not in the room and after some practice it will respond and come to you. You can reward your pet with a small treat when you train it to do this. If you teach your cat to come when you call it, it will also learn to overcome its shyness towards strangers, and some cats will go to anyone who calls their name.

Be gentle

Cats are very sensitive and pick up signals in your voice and touch. They can develop a deep fear of people if not treated with gentleness, especially if they are kittens.
Cats can sometimes get up to some really annoying antics, like playing tag on the computer keyboard. But it's always important to be very patient, scold with a gentle "no" and give a gentle pat on the butt.
Always be gentle with your pet when lifting and carrying. Provide lots of petting when they get frightened or come back after a visit to the vet.

Gain the trust of your pet

With consistent caution and patience, you can gain your cat's trust. When you bring a new cat home, keep her close and give her lots of cuddles and love. As she gets used to her new home, she will slowly start to explore.

Always take plenty of time to cuddle a new cat so she feels safe. You will know she trusts you completely when she lifts her head back while you gently stroke her chin. Exposing the sensitive neck area is a sign that your cat trusts you completely.

Arrange play dates with a cat-friendly puppy

Ideally, you should do this with a kitten or a very young cat. Cats are naturally suspicious of dogs, so this may not work with older cats. Introduce your kitten to a friendly puppy to encourage them to socialise. Please make sure the dog is cat friendly and used to being around cats. Cats and dogs make great pals when raised together, so if you like dogs and cats, this is something to consider.

Cuddle often

Sometimes we get caught up in our hectic, busy lives and tend to neglect our pets. Your cat will sense this and feel very down. She may either play extra cheeky tricks to get your attention or become very distant and depressed. Always make time for one or two daily cuddles with your pet, no matter how busy you are. She may not talk and tell you she misses you, but you can be sure she does. And as a member of the family, she deserves love and attention.

Final thoughts: While some breeds are naturally friendlier than others, all cats are naturally loving and affectionate. Follow the tips suggested here to get the best out of your pet and it will return the favour by bringing amazing joy to you and your family.

THE PERFECT CAT
FOOD

It goes without saying that you want your beloved pet to live a long, healthy life. Good health starts with good nutrition and that means a balanced diet that provides your cat with all the essential nutrients it needs. Follow these basic rules to ensure your pet gets the best nutrition.

Inculcate good eating habits

A cat is very persistent when it comes to food preferences, having decided what it likes and dislikes. It is best to introduce your pet to different foods at a young age to encourage them to develop a variety of preferences. Whether you use cat food or cook your cat's meals at home, help your kitty develop a taste for chicken, liver, meat, fish and vegetables. While some cats develop a preference for all foods, others prefer one or two, and that's perfectly fine as long as the meals are balanced and contain the right nutrients. Good eating habits also include regular meal and snack times. In general, the more structured your pet's eating habits are, the better.

Canned or dry food?

All vets recommend that you give your cat canned food at the main meals. Cats are carnivores and need a protein-rich diet to stay healthy and active. Unlike wet food, dry food contains less protein and more carbohydrates. However, they are fine as snacks or treats.

Like most pet owners, you will probably rely on store-bought cat food because you have a busy life. Just make sure you give her a nice selection, or at least the varieties she prefers.

Chicken is generally very popular with cats, but you can also give your cat other types of meat.

Make sure your cat's meals are balanced

Cat food manufacturers are required to follow strict regulations and most canned and dry cat foods contain everything your cat needs.

However, this is not always the case. Don't be impressed by fancy packaging or appealing pictures and slogans. Always read the labels on the cat food and look for a statement from the Association of American Feed Control Officials (AAFCO) or a similar body in your country confirming that the food meets the nutritional requirements for cats. This way you can be sure that your cat does not need any other vitamins or supplements.

When to feed your cat

When cats were wild predators thousands of years ago, they hunted at dawn and dusk, and that's when they ate. So basically, your cat is set to eat two main meals a day. These can be breakfast and dinner, with a light lunch of dry food, a boiled egg or other snacks.

Again, you will need to find out your cat's preferences, as some cats will forgo breakfast and prefer lunch and dinner as their main meals.

It is not recommended to feed your cat three large meals a day. Most cats won't say no, but remember that just like us humans, overfeeding can lead to obesity.

Can cats also eat human food?

Yes! Your kitty can eat a wide variety of human food and it's actually a good way to add variety to her diet.

Your pet can eat vegetables, boiled eggs, canned tuna, boiled meat. Poultry, liver, and even rice and pasta.

Of course, you should not use these foods as the main part of your pet's diet, but they are great as snacks or for an occasional lunch. You will also find that your cat has some quirky food preferences - all cats do. Cats are known to love watermelon, asparagus, French dried fruit and olives. So give your little friend a treat every now and then. It's completely safe.

Is home-cooked cat food healthy?

Homemade cat food is a nice change for in between. Every now and then I cook a chicken with potatoes and carrots, remove the bones and puree everything into bite-sized pieces. It's like a Christmas dinner for my cats - they just gobble it down.

If you want to make your pet an occasional home-cooked meal, you can find some great recipes for healthy cat food on YouTube.

What you should never feed your cats

While cats can safely eat almost all human foods, you should never feed them: Onions, garlic, chocolate, raw seafood, raw liver, caffeine, processed meat, bones and dog food! Also make sure that you do not feed raw eggs, as they sometimes contain disease-causing bacteria such as salmonella!

Pork is also strictly forbidden. It may contain the Aujeszky virus, which can cause a fatal disease of the nervous system, pseudo-rabies, in cats. The perfect diet for your cat requires no more than these basic steps. Get to know your cat's preferences for mealtimes and food choices, and together you will come to a perfect agreement. Stay consistent and let common sense prevail. Allow your pet occasional treats such as a piece of biscuit, a piece of watermelon or whatever their personal preferences may be. The result? A healthy, happy, well-fed cat.

SINGLE OR PAIR
HUSBANDRY?

One cat or two? This is a common question that pet owners ask themselves. If you are not yet a cat owner, should you choose one cat or a pair? If you already have a cat and get the feeling that it is lonely, should you get it a companion? And if you are thinking of two cats, should it be two males, two females or one of each?

There is no right or wrong answer. It is entirely up to you and depends on your family circumstances and preferences.

There are advantages and disadvantages to owning more than one cat. Here is a list of these to help you decide whether to have one, two or more cats!

Advantages

- As they get older, cats enjoy the company of other cats. They love to eat together, play together, groom each other and cuddle together during naps. If you already have a cat who is typically outgoing and friendly, a companion could be all she needs to make her happiness complete!

- Two or more cats make training easier. "Imitation" is the magic word here. Cats learn by watching and imitating each other. So two cats actually learn better than if you train them alone.

- Two cats help each other stay supple and active. Cats need exercise to stay fit and healthy. Of course, one cat can run, jump and be active on its own, but two give each other a super workout by playing tag, wrestling, high jumping and many more health-promoting cat exercises at lightning speed.

- If your cat is a picky eater, a companion can solve the problem. Firstly, her natural curiosity will make her try what her friend is eating. Secondly, the irresistible urge to copy may make her eat the same food as the other cat. This "peer pressure" from her companion will probably convince her to eat a more varied diet and overcome her pickiness.

- Cats make great pets because they can get used to being left at home while the family is away. But they can tend to get lonely if your schedule keeps you away from home all day. Having access to a backyard or garden can alleviate some of the boredom, but your pet will still be alone. This is a situation where you might want to consider adopting two cats.

- Cats that grow up in the company of other cats tend to be less shy, more playful and generally happier.

- When you adopt two or more cats, you provide a loving home for a kitten whose fate might otherwise be uncertain.

- Cat buddies look out for each other. I'm sure you've heard of the amazing stories where older cats have led their owners to lost kittens. That's right. These heroic deeds are not unique to dogs! A clever cat can actually save the day and save you a lot of heartache.

Disadvantages

- Two cats mean double expenses. This includes food, cat litter, vet bills and other cat stuff. The extra expense is not huge, but it is something to consider if you are on a tight budget.

- Two cats mean twice the cleaning effort. It means more cat hair and generally more effort to keep the house tidy and clean.

- Playing between two cats can be a bit rough, which means you need to take precautions such as keeping surfaces free of breakables, hiding power cables and keeping the bathroom door closed. Why the bathroom? In case your cats like to swing on the shower curtains like mine do! No matter how well trained, cats can forget themselves while having fun and do some damage. If you're in the house, a stern admonition will get them to calm down, but take precautions when you're not in the house, or leave them outside for the duration of the game.

Two things should be noted

1. It is much easier to adopt two kittens and raise them together. They will be best friends for life. Bringing a new addition into the family usually goes well. There may be some cautious hissing and growling from both cats, but if you hold them both and cuddle them, things will soon settle down and they will start to get to know each other.

For example, we tend to take in a lot of strays and what I have usually observed is that if the new cat is naturally shy, she can be bullied by the others at first. I make sure she gets extra attention and petting in front of the other cats. They soon realise that this is a special friend and amazingly they welcome him into the family very quickly. If your new cat is strong in character and outspoken, you needn't worry. He will quickly show all potential bullies who is boss.

The point is that it often happens that cats don't get along or fight fiercely. This is not something you need to worry about. Just keep an eye on them for the first few days and be ready to intervene if things get out of hand.

2. Which sex should you choose? It does not matter. Females get along well with other cats as well as with males. Male cats can make friends with both males and females. Apart from the mating behaviour already mentioned, cats get along with other cats as soon as they are neutered, regardless of gender.

Final thoughts:
Allow me to add my personal opinion here. It seems to me that the advantages far outweigh the disadvantages. I heartily recommend getting two cats. The extra effort and cost is negligible and the joy of seeing a great friendship develop between your pets is so worth it! How about more than two? If you are able, the more the merrier, I always say!

SOCIALISE CATS

Relationships are important, even for cats! Raising a social cat is important for its emotional health. Healthy emotional health is an essential complement to your cat's nutrition and fitness.

Cats that are shy, fearful or aggressive may have trouble socialising with other cats and forming bonds with people. Don't be fooled by your cat's behaviour. She may act like she's perfectly content doing things alone, but deep down, all cats want to interact and make friends. It is entirely possible to have the most popular cat in the neighbourhood if you teach her to socialise and develop healthy relationships with cats, dogs and you.

Signs that your cat needs to be socialised

- With people she knows, your cat is lively, lovable, affectionate and outgoing. But if strangers or other cats appear on the scene, she will run away and hide.

- When strangers or other cats try to be friendly, she becomes aggressive, growling and hissing.

- If she shows fear and distress in unfamiliar environments, such as the vet's surgery or car journeys.

Socialise kittens

Socialising a kitten is easy because like a baby, a kitten is discovering its new world and is usually very curious and excited to learn and explore. Kittens in a litter naturally learn to socialise because they are born with brothers or sisters with whom they play and wrestle in the cutest way. However, if this is not the case, you will need to teach your kitten this social behaviour.

- All you need to do is consistently introduce your kitten to new environments, new sounds, smells, people and other cats.

- Allow them to explore the outdoor area in an enclosure and when they are used to it, bring in a puppy or cat to play with them.

- Allow her to explore the interior, encourage her and stroke her often.

- Do not overtax her. Let her get familiar with things at her own pace and give her all the time she needs. Do this in small steps, introducing something new every few days. When this becomes the norm in a kitten's life, she can't help but become social and friendly.

Socialisation of an older cat

A moody or aggressive cat can learn to be social and friendly with a lot of positive reinforcement and patience. The steps are similar to training a kitten, but while a kitten is eager to explore, an older cat may need some coaxing.

- First, have your cat's favourite treat ready to reward and motivate her. She will respond better when she is hungry, so train her before a meal.

- When you pet your cat, try gently combing it with a cat brush. Most cats enjoy brushing. It is very relaxing and puts them in a good mood. They are also more accepting of being groomed by a companion and return the favour!

- Take your cat outside to an enclosure and let her explore a little. If she has toys, put them in the enclosure. Let your cat explore for a few minutes and then give her a treat. Always give her the treat by hand. After the treat, let your cat explore a little more and then give her another treat. 15 minutes should be enough for this training, but if your cat enjoys it, leave it a little longer.

- When you feel she is comfortable with the situation, perhaps a week later, and is no longer wary, introduce another cat. Allow them to get to know each other for a few minutes if it is a strange cat. Wait a few minutes and give them both a treat.

- Stay within sight of your cat and talk to it encouragingly.

- Take your cat to small gatherings where other cats or humans are present. Let her get used to human conversation, children playing and other different sounds and smells. Pet her reassuringly and talk in a soft voice to calm her down.

- Take your cat with you for short car rides. When you get home, give her a nice cuddle and a treat.

- Do daily play exercises with your cat. Keep her active by playing with her, letting her jump and throwing things to her to chase. Exercise reduces stress and helps your cat feel more relaxed and less moody or anxious.

- Patience! Older cats can take weeks to months to socialise and build relationships. Give your cat its own space and time and never scold or be impatient.

To conclude the chapter:
Cats can develop great relationships with other cats and people. If your cat is struggling in this area, cat socialisation training can help. If you are consistent and patient, you will gradually see an amazing change. It's worth the effort because your sweet friend deserves to love and be loved. Socialisation training will help her do this.

MEASURES &
APPROACHES

Whether you are house-training your cat, training its social behaviour or trying to correct a particular behaviour, there are some important rules you should follow.

What types of behaviour would you want to correct? Again, it depends on your pet's unique quirks. The most common are an obsession with scratching the furniture, being too aggressive in play, knocking things off shelves and going into a manic play mode in the middle of the night.

Some cat behaviours can be quite annoying. For someone like me who has several cats, they can be a challenge to reason with. Don't worry, all this can be corrected if you go about it the right way. Let's first look at what you need to avoid.

Do not shout or scream

Your cat will not associate the crying with the behaviour you are trying to break her of. She may get scared and run away, but as soon as you turn your back, she will go back to her fun. Save your breath and don't waste your time yelling and screaming. It will only scare your cat temporarily and if you overdo it, she will start to distrust and fear you.

Do not spray with water

I don't know who came up with this idea, but supposedly using a spray gun or spray bottle to wet your cat corrects bad behaviour. This is nonsense.

Once again, your cat will never associate this tactic with behaviour - but it will associate it with you. The only thing this will do is make your pet start to fear you and run away as soon as you approach. This can cause a major rift in your relationship and it will take a long time to regain your friend's trust in you.

Do not encourage bad behaviour

Everything kittens do is so adorable. We love it when they kick and nibble their tiny hind paws. We laugh and grab the camera when she grabs a sock or other object and somersaults across the floor to shred it.
By laughing and giving her a big "Aww!", we signal to the kitten that her behaviour is acceptable.
It won't be fun when she's older and those little nips become pretty painful bites! And we won't say "Aww!" when we find our favourite pair of shoes shredded either.
So smile to yourself and enjoy the moment, but don't let your kitten know by making encouraging sounds or picking him up and petting him.

Do not leave the house untidy

Having a pet means making a few sacrifices. This includes keeping the house as tidy as possible. Clear shelves of valuable items and keep small items out of your cat's reach. Try to keep your home as streamlined and minimalist as possible. The less clutter, the less mischief your cat can get into.

Do not use repellents

Never use mothballs or other repellents to keep your cat away from certain areas. These substances are highly toxic and should never be used anywhere in the house.

Do not punish

Never lock your cat in a room and never spank or nose it, no matter how gently. Time-outs or a gentle pat on the bottom are fine for children, but don't work for cats because they won't make the association. There is also a risk that you will traumatise them.

Instead, you should rather:

Provide toys

Cats play with shoes, toilet paper and knock things off shelves because they see them as toys. If you provide your cat with some stimulating toys, it is very likely that she will be busy and happy during playtime. She will gradually show less interest in your things and the behaviour will stop or become much less frequent. Remember to regularly supplement your cat's toys with something new to keep her interested.

Use an unpleasant odour

This is the right way to teach your cat to make an association between what she is doing and a smell she does not like. The unpleasant sensations will cause her to stop what she is doing and walk away. More importantly, she will not see you as the meanie who spoils all her fun!

So what smells do cats hate? There are sprays containing cat repellents sold in pet shops. They are made with artificial chemicals and are odourless to you but unpleasant to cats. There are also several natural scents you can try, such as citrus oil and clove oil. These are good natural cat repellents and are safe. Spray furniture, surfaces and other objects you want your cat to stay away from.

Invest in a cat tree

Cats scratch furniture and doorposts to mark their territory. A scratching post or even two will solve this problem. Your cat will fall in love with its scratching post and won't need anything else. Place the posts in places where your cat usually scratches and spray them with some catnip to make them more irresistible.

Cover surfaces with aluminium foil or plastic film

Cats do not like to walk on these materials and will stay away from surfaces where they are spread out. I used cling film on my kitchen counters, which my cats often jumped on. It wasn't great for me because I wanted my nice shiny worktops back, but I kept it up for a few weeks.

My cats would jump up on the worktops, walk around carefully and jump back down with a disgusted look. After about three weeks they gave it up completely and the behaviour stopped.

In conclusion: Understanding what works and what doesn't will save you a lot of time and frustration when training your cat. These basic rules should take care of curbing bad behaviour and instilling good habits.

Again, patience is the key. It may take weeks before you notice the first results, but be persistent. Remember that you and your furry friend need time to learn and adapt.

CONSISTENCY
AND POSITIVE
REINFORCEMENT

Let's start with a basic definition of positive reinforcement. It is something that motivates your cat to repeat a certain behaviour. However, positive reinforcement is not unique to cats. Children, adults, dogs and other animals also respond to positive reinforcement.

How is consistency related to this? Consistent positive reinforcement leads to consistent behaviour in our cat. When a certain behaviour is repeated consistently, it becomes a habit. The brain recognises that the repeated behaviour is desired and literally readjusts to make it a consistent habit.

Conversely, punishment and discipline are a form of negative reinforcement where certain behaviours are discouraged before they become habits.

Suppose you are training your cat to walk outside on a leash. Initially she may be anxious and try to get off the leash or run away. Bend down to pet her and say a few reassuring words to give her positive reinforcement. Similarly, picking your pet up for a cuddle before you put them on the leash is positive reinforcement.

In short, positive reinforcement teaches your cat good habits and also strengthens your relationship; you will enjoy rewarding your cat for good behaviour and he will love the extra attention. Read on to learn how to motivate your cat with positive reinforcement through rewards and how to use effective discipline.

HOW TO SCOLD
AND REWARD
PROPERLY

Training a cat is very similar to training a child, as it is based on two main pillars: Discipline and Reward. We have already touched on this, but now we want to go into more detail about what discipline and reward mean.

The most important thing is that you remain consistent with both methods so that your cat understands that you mean business. Good behaviour is praised and rewarded, while undesirable behaviour is not tolerated. Your clever cat will learn very quickly where its best interests lie, so to speak, which will make your task easier.

How to scold and discipline

There are 5 effective ways to discipline your cat when she gets out of hand. It is necessary to put your foot down when their behaviour is disruptive and worse, can put them in danger. A word of advice here: reserve these scolding techniques for times when they are really needed, so that your cat learns to associate scolding with serious problems. Constant scolding will either traumatise your pet or cause it to develop a thick skin and ignore you.

1. Use certain words

Create a small vocabulary of two or three words that you will consistently use to scold. Obviously, a stern "no" will be one of them. Other words could be "Ouch!", "Bad!", "Stop it!" or "Oh!". When scolding, always use these words so that your cat associates them with the unwanted behaviour.

2. Speak the name of your cat

Adding your cat's name to an admonition will make it clear that he is the little offender being addressed. "Bad Jax!" or "Jax, no!" will be much more effective, especially if your cat has learned her name.

3. Use a special scolding tone

Your tone of voice when scolding should be firm, calm and a little angry, but never harsh or loud, just negative enough to startle your cat and get its attention.

Your cat will learn that it means it is doing something it shouldn't, if you use this special tone, over time the unwanted behaviour will stop.

4. Remove your cat

When you separate your cat from an unwanted behaviour, you send the message that you are not happy with him. My cat Opie had a bad habit of eating from his companions' bowls. He would go from bowl to bowl and eat from everyone except his own. Needless to say, this irritated his companions and meals often became a melee of growling, hissing cats. I started to remove Opie from the feeding area and put him outside with his bowl. At first he was a little confused and stood meowing outside the door. I never let him get too distressed though. I brought him inside after the other cats had eaten and put his bowl in the designated place. After I had done this repeatedly, he eventually learned to let his companions eat in peace and to stick to his own bowl instead of being banished to the garden.

Removing your cat from the behaviour or situation is a great method of discipline. Just take her firmly in your hand, scold her and take her somewhere else. Touch her gently but firmly so she doesn't mistake your touch for a caress. She will soon get the message.

5. Be consistent

If you scold negative behaviour over and over again, your cat will think she can get away with it sometimes. Scold her every time she shows the behaviour so she takes you seriously.

How to reward

A good reward system is important to keep your cat motivated to learn and behave well. Observe your cat and identify its special triggers or preferences. This could be food, special playtime with you, cuddles or a favourite toy.

1. Rewards vary

Your cat will get bored if you always offer the same reward. Instead, keep her interested and motivated with a variety of rewards that you offer in turn. This nice selection of treats will keep them on their toes, while offering the same reward over and over again will cause a reward to lose its value - and therefore your cat will lose its motivation too.

2. Make rewards proportionate

You may want to save your cat's very special favourite treat for a very special behaviour. Most cats are crazy about tuna. A nice bowl of tuna sends the message that you are very pleased. She will surely remember the behaviour that earned the special treat and continue to do it.

3. Use lots of encouragement

Create a short vocabulary of praise words such as "Great job!", "Wow!" or other short statements of encouragement. Praise and encouragement will leave your pet on cloud nine. Combine these words back with their name and make sure your voice is warm, happy and excited.

4. Reward immediately

Offer your reward immediately when your cat has done something well, so keep your treat box handy. If the rewards are some playtime or petting. Initiate this immediately too. This avoids confusion in your cat and allows him to make a direct connection between a behaviour and the reward.

5. Measure your cat's mood

Match the rewards to your cat's mood to make them more motivating. If you are training after a wild playtime, food or cuddling is a better choice. After a nap or quiet time, a nice outdoor playtime with you and her toys is just what she needs,

Windfall profits

Disciplining negative behaviour and encouraging positive habits is probably something you will do over and over again for a long time. These simple techniques will enable you to train your cat as well as possible most of the time. Just remember that cats, are cats and mischief is in their blood. That's what makes them so lovable!

Kitten housetraining

This is the most important point for every pet owner. If there is one thing you need to get right, it is to house-train your pet as soon as possible. Fortunately, litter box training is fairly simple and straightforward and it is very rare for a cat to give you too much trouble. In fact, most cats get the hang of it quickly and quickly get used to using the litter tray without too much fuss. Cats are instinctively wired to bury their urine and faeces. When they lived in the wild, they did this to hide traces of their presence from predators, but also to protect their litters. For this reason, they sniff the litter box after going to the toilet to make sure they have completely covered the smell. In other words: Your cat prefers a litter tray and you, of course, completely agree! Of course, it is much easier to housebreak a kitten, but if you are taking in a stray or adopting an older cat that is not housebroken, the steps are the same but may require more time and patience. Here you will find all the tips you need to successfully housebreak your pet.

Litter tray and litter

Your pet's litter box should be at least 10 cm deep. It should be large enough for your kitten to fit in it as it grows. So the ideal size is one that an adult cat can manoeuvre and turn around in. An ideal choice is a litter tray that comes with a scoop and is very inexpensive.

The placement of the litter tray is important because it should stay in a fixed place so as not to confuse your cat. It should not be in the middle of the room, but placed in a corner or nook. Cats like privacy when they do their business, so this is another point of mutual agreement.

Type of litter: There are two types, clumping litter or non-clumping litter. The first type forms clumps with urine, which are ideally scooped out daily. The second type soaks up urine. To clean it, you only need to remove the faeces once or twice a day and stir the litter well. This type of litter lasts longer than the clumping litter. Try both types to see if your kitten prefers one. If it makes no difference to her, either type is fine.

Cat toilet training

As soon as you get home, put your cat or kitten in her litter tray. She will sniff it and if she doesn't have the urge, jump out again. But the introduction has already been made and registered in her memory, keep picking them up and putting them in the litter tray frequently.

Keep an eye on your kitten and if she starts sniffing or scratching the floor, quickly put her in the litter tray.

Expect a few accidents during training and keep a good, pet-friendly cleaner handy to clean up spills.

If your cat continues to ignore the litter tray, observe if he has another preferred place and is more likely to put the litter tray there.

If an older cat stubbornly ignores the litter tray, you can scold it using the methods discussed earlier.

If your kitten prefers to do her business on a carpet or other soft surface, gently bring her near the dirt so she can smell it, gently admonish her and take her to the litter tray. She will soon catch on.

Unfortunately, we often hear about crazy training methods, such as dipping the cat's nose in the dirt and yelling at it. Please never do something like that, no matter which animal.

You really shouldn't have any problems housebreaking your cat. Most cats can usually be housetrained within two or three days if you keep picking them up and putting them in the litter tray often. Once that's done, you can breathe a sigh of relief.

Breaking the habit of unpleasant behaviour

Your cat may have a mind of its own when it comes to training. She is often indifferent, unresponsive and downright stubborn. In fact, she seems to go out of her way to constantly contradict you. So, as a precaution, prepare to break the habit of disagreement with the following steps:

Use chuck

One of the most annoying habits of a cat is to refuse to come when called. It is also a sign of stubbornness if it happens repeatedly. You call and call, but she doesn't answer, even though she knows her name. You start to worry, thinking that something has happened to her, until eventually she saunters off to the litter tray or her water bowl. She often comes when she is called to eat and can smell the food. In this case, avoid calling her name except at mealtimes. Continue this for a few weeks until she associates her name with the food. Next, call her name when it's mealtime and give her a treat from your hand. Continue this for a few weeks to get her used to it,
This kind of training will break this annoying and worrying habit. Your cat will learn to come whenever you call it.

Ignore them

Ignore your cat for a few days. Don't pick her up and don't pet her. Just let her go about her day and only call her at mealtimes.

Chances are good that your cat will come to you! She may start to follow you timidly or even jump on your lap. In this case, shower her with love and positive reinforcement and all will be well!

Be persistent in training

Continue to train your cat with a combination of discipline and positive reinforcement and be persistent and patient. Even the most stubborn cats can be trained with patience, consistency and lots of love.

Final thoughts:
I have raised many super stubborn cats as well as very motivated and compliant cats and have loved them all equally. If your cat is stubborn, do your best to break the habit or at least partially break it. As long as you love her and she feels the same, you will find a way to live together in perfect harmony.

CLICKER
TRAINING

Some cats run like lightning when they hear the food bag coming out of the cupboard. My cat Opie runs to the door and meows when the sprinkler in the garden is turned on. He loves to run in and out of the sprinkler. Some very social cats come running when a doorbell rings.

The point is that some cats respond better to auditory signals than to verbal commands. For this reason, clicker training is very effective (when rewarded with a treat) in teaching your cat a variety of things.

The click sound helps the cat recognise the behaviour, while the treat confirms that the behaviour is desired. Clicker training is simple, fun for you and your pet, and very effective with most cats. Learn how to do clicker training in a few simple steps here:

Invest in a clock or choose a tone that you use consistently

Clickers are sold in pet shops and are cheap, but there is nothing special about them except that they make a clicking sound. You can imitate the sound with a biro, snap your fingers or cluck your tongue. The first step is to agree on a signal you want to use and stick to it.

Decide on the reward

This must be a very special treat. Only use this treat for clicker training so that it retains its high value for your cat. The best treat is usually a food that smells delicious to cats, such as a small piece of grilled fish, liver or tuna. It should be a food that your cat does not eat often.

Some professional cat trainers offer smoked turkey as a treat, and apparently cats love it.

Make sure the treat is small, so only give your cat one or two bites to leave him wanting more.

Use of the clicker

The aim is to let your cat know that the clicking sound it hears is associated with a heavenly treat.

Sit on the floor, place a bowl of covered treats next to you and your pet nearby.

Click once and give her a small bite of food. Click again and offer another treat and so on until the treats are used up. You have just started clicker training!

Continue this for about a week.

Associating with a behaviour

Watch your cat until you catch her doing something you want, e.g. sitting. As soon as she sits down, use the clicker, say "Sit" and offer a treat. Continue this every time your cat sits down.

After initial confusion, your cat will understand that "sit" is synonymous with "treat" and will sit down immediately when it hears the clicker.

The purpose of clicker training
Clicker training is typically used to teach cats tricks, but it can also be used for more useful behaviour, such as accepting a collar and leash, getting into a car, or getting into a carrier cage.

Final thoughts:
Don't be discouraged if your cat doesn't respond to clicker training as quickly as you would like. Clicker training can take some time. So don't focus on the end result, but enjoy this special time with your darling and have fun!

TEACHING CATS
TRICKS

If you want to teach your cat a few tricks for the amusement of family and friends, it is quite possible with clicker and command training. You can use the clicker to get your pet's attention, but you need to add a specific command like "sit", "jump", "kiss" and so on so that your cat can differentiate. If your cat responds easily to this type of training, you can teach him a number of adorable tricks that will delight your friends and fill you with pride in your clever kitty.

Here are some suggestions for some fun and delightful tricks. You can use a clicker for initial training, followed by a command until your cat learns to respond only to the command.

Shake hands

Hold up your cat's paw, click and say "Shake hands" and gently shake her paw. Give your cat a treat. Repeat the exercise every day for two to three minutes until your cat learns to give you her paw on command when you hold up your hand.

Jumping

Take your cat's treat between your fingers and hold it above its head. Click and say "jump". Most cats will jump to grab the treat. If your cat doesn't, bring it close to her nose so she can sniff it, lift it again and repeat the command. Repeat the exercise daily for 2-3 minutes until your cat learns to jump on command without the clicker.

Give a kiss

Use a treat that you can apply to your face, e.g. cream cheese, cream, yoghurt or baby food in your cat's favourite meat. Dab a small piece on your cheek. Sit your pet on your lap and say "Kiss!". Lower your face and repeat the command for your cat to lick the food.

Repeat the training every day for about 2-3 minutes and gradually stop lowering your face, but coax your pet to stand on your lap and lick the food off your cheek.

Finally, ask your pet for a kiss without food on its face to confirm that it has learned how to give a kiss. Aww!

Give a high five

This trick may be easier if you have already taught your pet to shake hands. Hold your cat's paw at the level of her head and say "high five", touching her paw with your hand. Offer a treat and repeat.

Repeat this daily for 2-3 minutes until your cat can high-five like a pro!

Note: Remember to offer a treat after you have triggered a command to motivate your cat.

I think you have an idea of how to teach your cat some cute tricks. You can use the same method to teach her to stand, sit, retrieve and jump. Again, be consistent, and have fun!

AT THE END

Adopting a cat is like bringing a new baby home from the hospital. As soon as you step through the door, she is officially a new member of the family. As such, she deserves everything a family member deserves, including great discipline and training.

I hope this book has given you an insight into common cat behaviours so that you and your cat can learn to get along well. I hope you found it entertaining and informative. Most importantly, I hope I have given you the tools you need to help your cat be the best and happiest he can be!
Raising your sweet pet to be social, well-behaved and friendly is a labour of love that will serve him well for the rest of his life. If you do this with heart, love and patience, you can be sure that you will raise a great pet.
The pride and love you will feel for your pet as it blossoms and your relationship grows stronger is indescribable. Raising a cat can be a life-changing experience. It certainly was for me and it has brought me incredible joy and inner peace. In today's manic world of greed, slander and materialism, we can often lose our sense of purpose. We overlook the things that really matter. But after a crazy day, when your precious pet curls up contentedly purring in your lap, you realise that it's moments like these that really count.

✝

19 March 2021

In loving memory of Opie

Printed in Great Britain
by Amazon

17744756R00047